Known Only Unto God

This is the story of the author's grandfather, Frank Ellis, a country boy from North Hertfordshire who, along with thousands of other patriots, answered the call of Lord Kitchener and joined the army in 1914.

Times were hard and the lure of the excitement of war, a secure job where food and accommodation was provided and the pride of wearing a uniform was hard to resist.

Frank spent two years training and fighting for his country, first of all in Flanders and then at the Somme where he lost his life.

Most of the time in the trenches he lived like an animal – nearly always wet and filthy, eating, sleeping and fighting in the mud and slime, sharing a hole in the ground with rats, slugs, frogs and beetles.

The stench of death was always present as he lived alongside the decaying corpses of his fallen colleagues.

Frank's body was never identified and his final resting place is Known Only Unto God.

Other titles by Doug Ellis:-

'Travels in South America'

'Jimmy in the Jungle'

Copyright © 2014 Doug Ellis

Doug Ellis has asserted his right under the Copyright, Design and Patents Act 1988 to be identified as the author of this work.

Known Only Unto God

Doug Ellis

"If I should die, think only this of me:

That there's some corner of a foreign field.

That is forever England."

Rupert Brooke 1887-1914

1877 – Frank's parents.

Bill and Annis Ellis lived in the small village of Norton in the north of Hertfordshire, surrounded by rolling countryside given over mainly to growing barley, wheat and oats. In fact Bill had been born and had lived all of his twenty-one years in Norton – living in the same tiny thatched cottage and working as a farm labourer since he was fourteen years old for the local squire Hugh Pym.

The Pym family owned most of the land around Norton and some of the other local villages and were the principal suppliers of barley to the local brewery, Simpson's, in the nearby market town of Baldock. The barley was malted in the many maltings scattered around Baldock and was then used as an integral part of the process of making beer. The majority of the able bodied men in Norton worked in some way or another for the Pyms.

As a farm labourer Bill's life was a hard one; in the summer the days were long and the work, particularly at harvest time, was tiring when there always seemed to be a rush to get the corn cut and stacked before the rains came to spoil it. This was a time of long back-breaking hours, from sunrise to sunset in the heat and dust of the fields where Bill would spend most of his time cutting corn, swinging a heavy scythe all day long. At harvest time Bill worked from six in the morning until eight at night. The rest of the summer he worked from six until six.

Once the corn was cut those women who worked on the farm would follow behind gathering up the cut stalks into small sheaves. Men then followed the women and shocked the sheaves collecting ten together to form a shock ready for the horse and cart to pass by when they were pitchforked up onto the cart – this was very heavy work.

After the sheaves had been carted to the barn they would be laid out on the clay-daub floor and the big doors at each end of the barn would be opened to encourage a through draught.

The threshing was done by hand with wooden flails; a three or four foot long handle of ash with a swivel at the top. Another piece of wood, normally of holly or blackthorn was connected to the swivel and secured with a snakeskin. This second piece of wood had to be brought down hard on the sheaves striking the corn just below the grains so that they would be released from the ear but not bruised.

Sievers would then sort out the grain from the chaff and the threshed corn would be thrown high in the air with a flat wooden shovel known as a scuppit. The heavier grains would settle close to the thrower and the dusty pieces and broken grains would fly further away. The inferior grains, the tailings, were given to the animals as feed.

At midday Bill's wife Annis would walk down to the fields where he was working carrying a basket with couple of slices of bread and if he was lucky a piece of cheese or fatty bacon for his lunch. This was usually washed down with water but occasionally she would bring a small jug of beer from The Three Horseshoes pub just down the road if their finances could run to it.

During the winter months the days were shorter and the work was different, mainly clearing out the many ditches around the fields, mending fences, cutting wood and generally tidying up around the farm. The main problem in the winter was that he had to spend all day outside in the cold, in the rain, snow, hail and sleet and often in temperatures below freezing with no really warm clothes to keep the weather out. The working day at this time of year was from seven in the morning until five at night.

If Bill became ill or for any reason was unable to work he didn't get paid and as the house went with the job he tried to keep his employer happy. If you were unemployed you were automatically homeless.

Bill's father had also worked for the Pyms and the house had been occupied by the Ellis family for three generations – Bill wasn't going to give this up easily so often he would work when he was feeling under the weather and suffered even more than usual. The days were just work and bed, work and bed; he was too tired most of the time for much else.

A normal working week was six days but at harvest time they would be expected to work on Sundays too if the harvest demanded it. Bill wasn't a churchgoer and his only free day was more often than not spent cultivating a small vegetable patch at the rear of the cottage where he was able to grow a few fresh vegetables to supplement their meagre diet.

For breakfast, which would normally be taken around five o'clock, Annis would rustle up a bowl of porridge and a cup of tea. In the evening it was mainly potatoes, a few greens from the garden and bread. On the few occasions when they ate meat it was usually a rabbit that Bill had snared on a Sunday. Sometimes he would meet up with George who was a local poacher and he would sell Bill a pheasant or partridge from the local estate – but Bill could usually not afford such a luxury.

There was no oven in the cottage so everything was boiled in a black cast-iron pot that hung above the log fire in the open fireplace and the meals were sometimes padded out by the addition of wheat or barley grains.

The cottage that came with the job was one in a row of four such cottages in Church Street just along from St. Nicholas' church. There were two small rooms upstairs which served as bedrooms and two rooms downstairs; the larger of the downstairs rooms was the living room with a small scullery at the back.

The walls were constructed of timber frames with a lath and plaster infill between. In places the plaster had broken away and daylight could be seen through some of the cracks and holes. The walls were very thin and as such the house was cold and draughty during the winter months. The roof was thatched and was generally in need of repair although it didn't leak too much and the bedrooms were reasonable dry although cold.

The floor downstairs was of compacted earth and the wooden floorboards upstairs had gaps between them and dust would fall down from above into the living room and the scullery.

Upstairs you could see the underside of the straw of the thatch and this was always home to a few mice – birds made their nests in the outside part of the thatch.

There was no running water in the house but the row of cottages did have a pump just down the road and Annis would carry water from there in a bucket. As there was no bath they took it in turns to wash in a wide washbasin on the rickety table in the scullery. Only in the depths of freezing winter did they treat themselves to the luxury of some hot water heated over the fire. The slops from the washbasin would be thrown out into the garden at the back to water what vegetables there were.

There was a privy or toilet at the top of the small garden; just a small wooden shed with a deep hole covered with a wooden box seat with two holes in it – no one thought anything of having someone else sitting at their side while they did their business in the morning. About once a year a man was called in from Baldock to clean out the privy. There was a hatch outside which opened out into the hole beneath the toilet and with a long-handled flat spade he would shovel out the accumulated excrement into a large container which he took away on his cart. This was a day for all the children to come out to watch, grimace, pull faces and screw up their noses.

Bill and Annis had started courting over two years before – mainly walking out together through the local lanes or down to the River Ivel at Norton Fisheries where they would lie on the banks during the long summer evenings listening to the birdsong, watching the kingfishers diving into the water and emerging with small fish in their mouths, larking around in the shallow waters of the brook and generally trying to forget the harsh daily routine of work.

There was no spare money to indulge in even small presents for one another but this wasn't expected and they enjoyed one another's company and before long they were having sex on a more or less regular basis. This usually occurred on a soft bed of hay in one of squire Pym's barns.

In the early months of 1875 Annis realised that she was pregnant – there were no contraceptives available to a lowly farm worker in those days. The couple would get married as it was unthinkable and financially impractical for a girl to bring up a child on her own – there was also the question of the social stigma that would be attached to such a scenario.

Bill was nineteen and Annis was twenty two when they became married in April 1875 at Saint Nicholas' church with the Reverend Pierson presiding – a simple ceremony, no special clothes, just their best things cleaned up and patched where necessary. Saint Nicholas' church in Norton was to witness many christenings, marriages and deaths of the Ellis family for years to come.

Their friends clubbed together and took them down to The Three Horseshoes for a drink after the ceremony to celebrate; but that was all. The next day Bill was back at work clearing out ditches in the drizzling rain – mud up to the top of his boots and rain running down the back of his neck.

His meagre wages would now have to support an extra mouth.

Their first child, William Henry, but know to everyone as Billy, was born in October of that year; a fine strong, healthy boy who would no doubt grow up to follow in his father's footsteps on the farm.

Billy was two years old now and Bill and Annis had managed to avoid having other children up until that point.

But throughout the harvest of 1877 Annis became progressively more and more uncomfortable with the new child that was growing inside her. Nevertheless, she at least carried on plaiting straw to earn a little bit of extra income. The plaited straw was used in the manufacture of straw hats, (boaters), at nearby Luton which was the centre of the hatter's trade in England at that time.

Most of the wives and many of the young girls in Norton would spend several hours each day plaiting lengths of straw which were collected every fortnight by Mr Kingsley who came around all the local villages with his horse and cart picking up the straw plaits and paying cash in return.

Both Bill and Annis were very happy to think that they would be having another child, but at the back of their minds was the worry of just how they were going to manage financially.

The summer wore on and Annis, although in good health generally, became more and more weary and irritable with Bill. They didn't know when the baby was due as there was no question of consulting a doctor on such an everyday event as having a baby, but by the end of August it was clear that the birth was not too far away.

September 15th 1877.

'Mrs Izzard, Mrs Izzard come quick. I've started.'

'Alright dear. Hang on, I'm coming round.'

Mrs Izzard lived next door to the Ellis family and had no trouble hearing Annis' cries for help through the paper-thin walls that divided the cottages.

'My waters have just broken Mrs Izzard, so it won't be long now.'

'Let's get you upstairs then Dear – nice and easy does it; then I'll run down to the village and get Mrs Perkins.'

Mrs Perkins was the equivalent of the local midwife and although she had no formal qualifications she had administered at more births in the village of Norton than she could remember.

Once Mrs Izzard had removed Annis' outer clothing she got her to lie on the bed and then left her and set off towards the village in search of Mrs Perkins.

In twenty minutes or so the two of them had returned to find that Annis' labour pains had become more regular, more frequent and more painful.

'Let's get young Billy next door for a while; our Mary can look after him for a bit,' said Mrs Izzard.

Meanwhile Mrs Perkins busied herself tearing up old sheets and getting the large cast-iron cooking pot filled with water to hang above the fire. By the time she had put more wood on the fire to get a good blaze going she could hear Annis' cries of pain from upstairs.

Mrs Perkins now came into her own telling Annis when to push and when to try to relax before the next contraction came.

'Shall we send word down to the farm to get Bill back here as it won't be very long now you know?' asked Mrs Perkins.

'No, don't bother – he won't be much help here will he? Let's get on with it and tell him when it's all over.'

The labour lasted three hours in all and Annis coped pretty well – after all more or less every other woman in the street had given birth to several children and this was only Annis' second, so she'd better not make too much fuss or it would be all around the village in no time.

No doubt there would be several more children to give birth to before her childbearing days were over.

At three o'clock in the afternoon out popped a healthy, bouncing boy.

'What is it Mrs Perkins?'

'It's a boy Annis, a lovely strong boy.'

'Is he alright?'

'He looks fine to me.' said Mrs Perkins as she cut the umbilical cord, lifted the baby aloft by his feet and gave him a resounding slap on the backside to make him cry which he did with a vengeance.

'What will you call him Annis?'

'We decided that if it was a boy we'd call him Frederick Francis.'

And so, Frederick Francis Ellis came into this world on the afternoon of 15th September in the year of 1877.

FRANK'S STORY.

The Early Years.

I'm Frederick Francis Ellis although everybody calls me Frank, or Frankie when I was little.

Obviously I don't remember what you've just been reading about – in fact I don't remember the first few years that I spent at Norton at all.

You see, a year after Mum had me, my eldest sister Beatrice was born and then a couple of years after that Mum became pregnant again. So by the year 1880 when I was three years old there were five of us in the small cottage in Norton and it really just wasn't big enough for all of us and the new baby that was on the way.

Luckily for us, Mr Pym, who was the village squire and Dad's employer must have thought very highly of my Dad as he offered him a bigger house that was one of several that he owned in Bygrave, a smaller village than Norton about two and a half miles away as the crow flies.

Mr Pym owned lots of land and lots of cottages in the area.

I can just about remember the day we moved – it would have been on a Sunday as that was the only day that Dad had off work, apart from the three days that were public holidays; Good Friday, Shrove Tuesday and Christmas Day.

We loaded all our worldly possessions, not that there so many of them, onto a handcart that Dad had borrowed from Mr Pym's farm manager. There was Mum and Dad's bed, the sacking mattresses stuffed with straw that we children slept on, a small cupboard where we kept our clothes and a few pots and pans including the big black metal cauldron in which most of our meals were cooked over the fire. There were a number of plates and cups and that was about it really apart from our clothes, most of which we were wearing on the day we moved.

Billy and me rode on top of all the things piled up on the cart and Mum walked behind carrying baby Beatrice. Although it was just over two miles in a straight line to Bygrave we couldn't go that way as the cart wouldn't go across the rough fields loaded up as it was. So we had to follow the road down to Baldock as far as the railway station and then from there to Bygrave which made it around four miles in all. I remember seeing a train cross over the bridge on Biggleswade Road and I was spellbound by the plumes of smoke coming up from its chimney and the chuffing noise it made as it pulled into Baldock station.

At first the going had been mainly downhill and we got on well but from Baldock onwards the road started to go uphill and the last bit up to Bygrave village was quite steep. Dad made Billy and me get off the cart and we had to help push – I don't think we helped much but at least Dad didn't have to push our weight as well.

Mum was heavily pregnant at the time and what with having to carry little Beatrice she kept lagging behind and was well and truly tired by the time we arrived in Bygrave. Billy and me were excited to see our new home which in fact turned out to be not very much different from the one we had just left in Norton. Thing was though that it did have more space upstairs and so the sleeping arrangements would be better.

The one large room upstairs was divided up into two areas with an assortment of odd pieces of material that acted as curtains. One area was for Mum, Dad and Beatrice and the other for Billy and me.

Bygrave was a much smaller village than Norton and had no pub and no shops. There was just the church, the manor and a few scattered cottages, one of which was ours. There were several children in most of the families there and so Billy and me soon made a few friends.

Dad still had to go to Norton to work each day on the same farm as before and so he had to get up even earlier every day and often set off across the fields in the dark and got back home in the evening often in the dark too during the winter; five miles a day walking on top of a long hard day's work. It wasn't really surprising that Dad never had much time to spend with us kids when he got home as he was always exhausted and just wanted to eat his dinner and then put his feet up although he did give us some time on Sundays when he wasn't pottering around in his vegetable patch.

Billy and me usually used to play out in the fields and in the woods near to the manor, which wasn't far from our cottage. We would sometimes get up to mischief but generally amused ourselves just messing around. I remember that we would sometimes find pheasant's nests loaded with a dozen or so eggs – they were usually on the edge of the woods and were strictly speaking the responsibility of the gamekeeper, Mr Matthews. We would sometimes take four or five eggs and run back home for Mum to cook them for us, with a nice piece of bacon if we were lucky, but usually it was just the eggs – fresh fried pheasant's eggs - wonderful. I can almost taste them now just thinking about it.

We had to be careful though not to run across Mr Matthews who regularly patrolled the area with his shotgun. We used to call him Golly Eyes on account of the thick glasses he wore. The lenses were like the bottom of jam jars and made his eyes look very big. If he saw us anywhere near the woods he would shout out loudly and we would scurry off home, scared out of our wits and half expecting that he would shoot us in the back as we ran away.

Every Wednesday morning we used to walk down to Baldock with Mum to the market where she did what shopping she needed; this wasn't usually very much to be honest although I don't know whether that was because we didn't have much money or because we didn't really need so much. The main ingredients of our diet were the vegetables that Dad grew in the garden or those that had been given to us by the neighbours when there was a glut.

Mum always bought fresh fish from a stall on the market – usually a nice herring for Dad's tea when he got home. Billy and me weren't too keen on herrings as we couldn't be bothered with all them bones – sometimes though it would be a mackerel which Mum would souse in vinegar or a few sprats which would be fried.

Mum would always go into the butcher's shop but sometimes would come out empty handed if it was too expensive. Sometimes though she would buy a few scraps of the cheaper fatty meat, usually pork or sometimes scrag-end of mutton and that was a great treat for us.

Billy and me always got an extra treat of a gobstopper or a stick of liquorice when we went into Mrs Juff's shop to get some tobacco for Dad – the sweets were all kept in large glass jars arranged in rows on the shelves that ran around most of the shop. Our eyes popped out of our heads looking at all the goodies in front of us but somehow we always chose a gobstopper or a stick of liquorice. We had to help carry the shopping home and we were usually complaining and dragging our feet by the time we got as far as Bygrave hill.

Not that long after we'd set up home in Bygrave Billy started going to school. He had to walk all the way to Baldock to the school in Park Street; Mum took him for the first week but after that he went with three or four other kids from the village and I was sad to see him go off with his new mates.

So suddenly I was on my own during the day with just Mum and my two small sisters Beatrice and Amy - Amy had been born in 1880. I had a couple of mates to play with when I wanted to but it wasn't quite the same as being with my big brother Billy.

The next year though, I started school myself and so I walked each day to Baldock and back with Billy – at first I thought that this was great as I was now a 'big boy' like Billy but it soon became a bit of a chore and I never liked the long walk to Baldock and back – especially when it was pouring with rain.

I was in Mr Humphries' class and although he was very strict he was alright really if you behaved yourself which I normally did.

The schoolwork consisted of us learning to read and write and reciting our times tables to give us a basic idea of maths. It all seemed a bit pointless to me at the time as we didn't have any books in the house to read and I didn't know anyone outside the village that I would want to write to. It was almost certain that I would follow in my Dad's footsteps and work on the farm where this sort of thing didn't seem to be necessary.

We didn't have any paper exercise books to work with in those days but each pupil had a slate on which we could practise writing – if there weren't enough slates to go around there were a few flat boxes filled with sand and we could write the letters of the alphabet in these.

On our way to and from school we used to pass by the brewery in the High Street – there was always a lovely smell coming from the brewery and it seemed to give a particular odour to the whole of the town.

Billy and me used to stand outside the brewery watching the horse drawn carts pull up outside laden with sacks. There was a little projecting cabin high up in the building and when the carts with the sacks arrived a long rope would descend down to the ground. The man in charge of the horse and cart would then hook the rope around one of the sacks and on a signal to the heavens above the sack would slowly rise up in the air.

When it got up to the little cabin a trapdoor would open and the sack would disappear inside. We used to stand there for ages watching this.

Horses and carts would also be coming out of the brewery all the time loaded up with barrels of beer that they were taking to the pubs around the town – there were more than twenty pubs in Baldock at that time. We would stand well back as they came out through the wide gates as we were a bit afraid that the massive shire horses that pulled the carts would step on us.

By the time I was seven Mum was pregnant again and my younger brother George was born in 1884. Billy was eleven by now and had started to do odd jobs at Manor Farm in the village. He earned a few coppers from picking up stones from the fields, helping to clear out ditches and keeping an eye on a few animals as they were grazing.

Then two years later Mum had yet another baby, my sister Maud, and so things started to get crowded again at home and we were constantly on top of one another. Six children and two grownups meant that we needed to move again to give ourselves more space.

Baldock and Edmonton.

As luck would have it, Dad heard about a cottage that was available in Baldock. We were excited to hear that we would be moving to what to us was a large town and more importantly for us children, no more walking five miles a day to school and back.

The cottage was in Chequers Yard at the back of the Chequers pub in Whitehorse Street. It was one of two such cottages in a small courtyard where horses and carriages had come in through a large arched entrance in days gone by. The cottages had probably been used for accommodation for travellers passing along the Great North Road, which was an important route from London to the North of England and Scotland.

There were shops within a few yards of our new home, a malting almost next door and of course we were always intrigued to peer in through the pub windows at night to see what was going on inside – we were never allowed in there though.

The pub, like most of the other pubs in the town, always seemed to be full of revellers during the evenings. There were rows of wooden tables in the single bar with wooden benches. Beer, which is what everyone seemed to drink, was drawn from the barrels into large jugs and these were taken around the tables to top up the customer's glasses as they became empty. There was a general hubbub of noise and laughter and we could usually hear this throughout the evening from our cottages.

Not many of the locals would eat at the pub but if there were travellers who were perhaps staying the night then they would be served with a simple meal, usually bread with a couple of slices of meat and a plate of cheese.

 The best thing of all though about living in Baldock for us children was that the school was only just up the road a quarter of a mile away and so we didn't have to get up quite so early in the mornings, nor did we have that long walk from Bygrave through the rain and snow in the winter.

Although the cottage was bigger than the one at Bygrave it was still very cramped, so when I was twelve years old my parents decided that it would be best for me if I were to go and live with my Uncle George and Aunt Isabella down in Edmonton to the north of London.

My Uncle George ran a florists shop in the town and I was to work as his assistant – I saw this as an easier option than becoming a farm labourer which is what Billy had become by this time. I wasn't too keen to leave the family but Mum and Dad explained that it would all be for the best and that I should look forward to it as a bit of an adventure and a change from what I'd been used to.

Uncle George was Mum's brother, his surname was Grey and they had no children and lived in a proper brick house at 37, Windmill Road in what I thought was a rather posh area. The house was much bigger than our little cottage in Chequers Yard and I even had my own bedroom for the first time in my life. There was so much space that Uncle George also took in a lodger, his name was Dave Gladley and he originally also came from Norton like me, but he now worked on a farm near Edmonton.

Uncle George's house was one in a terraced row of similar houses built with light coloured yellowish grey bricks. It had a nice bay window in the living room that looked out to the street and I used to like to sit by the window and watch the world go by.

I walked to the shop each morning with Uncle George – it was only a few roads away from Uncle's house - and I helped out in the shop, mainly unloading boxes of flowers that would be delivered by horse and cart direct from the big flower market in London. I would also have to clear up all the rubbish, sweep up and keep the place clean and tidy. I was never allowed to deal with the customers direct though as this was Uncle George's job

– he was a bit of a smooth talker and liked to chat with the ladies who made up most of our customers.

The work was easy but not very interesting to me and I missed the outdoor life if I'm honest. Then again, Uncle George didn't pay me very much as he provided me with my lodgings and Aunt Isabella cooked all my meals. I didn't need so much money really, but as I became older and started to go down to the Red Lion pub at the weekends, I soon realized that most of the other lads had more money than I did and they were able to treat themselves to some of the little luxuries in life that were denied to me.

One of the chaps that I used to have a pint with on a Saturday night was Henry Scales and he worked as a bricklayer. There was a lot of building work going on at that time and he said that he could get me a job working with him whereby I could learn a trade. Having thought about it for several weeks I eventually decided to give it a try as I thought that to have a trade behind me would ensure a steady flow of work and it was clear to me that a bricklayer certainly earned far more than a florist's assistant.

Uncle George wasn't too happy when I finally plucked up the courage to tell him that I would be finishing the job with him and although he didn't exactly throw me out, he did suggest that I should find somewhere of my own to live – I think he thought that I was being a bit ungrateful for what he had done for me but I felt the need to move on.

There was a spare room at the house where Henry lodged, it was just down the road at number 47 and so I moved in there. It was only six doors down from Uncle's house so we were able to stay in touch and I'm sure he let Mum and Dad know how I was now and then.

For the first few months my job on the building site consisted of mixing up cement by hand, wheeling heavy barrows around and the most difficult thing of all, carrying buckets of mortar up rickety ladders to the skilled bricklayers who were working high up on the scaffold.

I think this extremely hard and repetitive work was given to me at the beginning to see if I was strong enough to take it and to see if I would last the pace. I did and before long I found that I was far fitter than I had been before and I was by now enjoying my chosen vocation.

Eventually my workmates began to teach me the craft of laying bricks and within a couple of years I was able to lay a straight course and I was gradually able to build up my speed. I had to learn all the different ways of bonding the bricks together; Flemish bond, English bond and Rat-trap bond, they all needed different techniques. Walls were also of varying thicknesses and I had to learn how to lay the bricks to achieve this.

As I was now having to pay for my board and food the extra money that I was earning soon went and I found that I wasn't as well-off as I thought that I would be. Still, I managed alright and at least I now started to have some sort of social life in Edmonton.

I Get Married.

At the weekends I would sometimes go to dances in Silver Street in the middle of the town and although I wasn't much of a dancer it was here that Henry and I used to chat up the girls. I met Ellen Mary Smith at one of the dances in 1902 by which time I was twenty-four years old.

1902 was also the year of the big smallpox epidemic and that was very scary. Most of the people who contracted the disease in Edmonton came from the Victoria Road area, which was only a few streets over from Windmill Road where we lived. They built a temporary wooden isolation hospital in the town along Picketts Lock Lane and we were always keen to avoid going anywhere near that place in case we caught something nasty.

Edmonton was surrounded by countryside in those days and Ellen Mary and I would walk out across the fields at weekends or sometimes meet up in town with one or two friends. Ellen Mary lived at Fairbourne Road in Tottenham, which was only just down the road from my digs so we saw quite a bit of each other when she could slip out of the house.

It was in May of 1902 that we celebrated the first of the Empire Days, an annual celebration that was to continue for many years. They set up maypoles in the streets and a carnival atmosphere pervaded the whole town. We were proud to be part of the greatest Empire the world had ever known and it also meant that we all had a day off work.

By the end of 1903 we realized that Ellen Mary was pregnant and so we had to organise a hastily arranged marriage - this took place on 13th February 1904 by which time my new wife was six months gone.

We were married at All Hallows Church in Tottenham, Ellen's local church and I was really pleased that my sister Beatrice made the trip down to be a witness. Beatrice had got married to Bill Limmer just a couple of months earlier so we were both starting off in married life at about the same time.

Ellen Mary and I took up lodgings in Silver Street in February and on 4th May of the same year our first son William Frederick was born – named after my Dad and myself. I continued to work as a bricklayer as there was still plenty of work around as most of the suburbs were expanding around London.

Everything was going well for us; I had regular work, we had a lovely son in Billy, our rented house, just a couple of rooms actually, was simple but clean and tidy and Ellen Mary was able to earn a bit of extra pocket money by doing some sewing work for a few people in the area who were pretty well off and could afford to pay someone else to do this for them.

Two years later Ellen Mary was pregnant again and our second son, Leonard Frank Ellis, was born at Silver Street on 24th June 1906.

Back to Chequers Yard, Baldock.

In 1908 my father got in touch with us to say that the cottage next door to them in Chequers Yard was to become empty and would we be interested to move back to Baldock. Well, apart from Uncle George and Aunt Isabella, neither of whom we saw very often at that time, we didn't have any close relatives in the Edmonton area, so we decided that it would be good to move back alongside the family. I was fairly confident that I could still get work on building sites around Baldock so I handed in my notice and we upped sticks and move back north to Hertfordshire.

It wasn't long after we had arrived back in Baldock when we realized that Ellen Mary was pregnant yet again and our first daughter Dorothy Frances was born on 30th December 1908. There were now five of us living in the small cottage and next door were Dad and Mum who lived with my brothers George and Bert and my youngest sister Maude. Chequers Yard had really been taken over by the Ellis family.

Dad was now fifty-five years old and was working as a postman; he'd also managed to get Bert a job as a messenger boy at the post office, Bert was sixteen by now. My other brother George, who was twenty-six years old, worked as a general labourer, often on the same building sites as me. With such a big family it was handy to be living next to my parents and my siblings as this meant that there was always someone around to help out looking after the children if Ellen Mary and me ever needed to have a bit of time to ourselves.

The two 'Ellis cottages' became interchangeable insomuch that the children were as likely to be found in one cottage as the other. They also often ended up spending the night in whichever cottage they happened to fall asleep in that evening.

As it turned out, work for me on the building sites was far more difficult to be had in the Baldock area. In Edmonton and the surrounding areas there was still a lot of expansion going on to extend London further to the north and as such lots of houses were being built. It wasn't the same in Baldock where the population was not growing and the main focus for work, as it always had been, was agriculture and the local brewery Simpson's.

There were times therefore when I was out of work but then with the family all around us in Chequers Yard there always seemed to be at least one member who was bringing in a wage and so we were able to eke out the food and make sure that no one went hungry.

In 1912 Mary Ellen had another son who we named Leslie and so you can see that Chequers Yard was beginning to get rather crowded again although it was nice in some ways to have lots of children running around.

The street outside, Whitehorse Street, wasn't usually very busy and the children would play in the road quite a bit although it was actually the Great North Road running from London up to Scotland. There weren't so many motorcars in those days as mostly the roads were taken up with horses and carts and the children could always get out of the way of those.

I remember that one day Bill and Frank got hold of one of those wicker bath chairs that invalids use, (two wheels at the back and a single steerable wheel at the front) – don't know where they got it from – and they would take it in turns to ride down the hill on Royston Road and shoot over the crossroads at the bottom. I gave them a bit of a telling off when I got to hear about it, but I don't think they were really in very much danger.

Ellen Mary was expecting her fifth child as we moved into 1914 and things were getting harder for us all as a family. Christobel, our second daughter, was born in June by which time I was becoming increasingly concerned about whether or not I could earn enough to support my growing family.

The main employer in Baldock was still the brewery in the High Street and occasionally I would get some part-time work there when there was nothing to be had on the building sites, but even they had fewer jobs to go around than there were men looking for work.

We didn't take a newspaper in the house and there was no real means of keeping up with what was going on in the big wide world outside of Baldock. Fortunately though we had the pub, The Chequers, right next to our cottages and so gossip of what was happening in the country as a whole and to some extent abroad filtered down to us through the talk in the public bar.

By the time that 1914 had arrived it was clear that the politicians were rather pessimistic about what was happening in Europe and although to be quite honest most of it was above my head, it did seem that there was a possibility of a war in Europe. That didn't seem to concern us, as there was not much chance that any of us would ever go outside of England – after all, I'd never even been to London!

Anyway, it turned out that the rumours were right as in August 1914 someone that we'd never heard of before, Archduke Ferdinand, was killed by a man from Serbia, wherever that was, and this prompted Britain to declare war on Germany.

We still didn't think at the time that this would have any effect on us but as the weeks rolled by after the declaration of war, it seems that they suddenly realised that Britain just didn't have enough soldiers to put up against the Germans and Lord Kitchener, who was in charge of the army, started a campaign to drum up more recruits.

A wave of patriotism seemed to flow across the country as people from all walks of life decided to join up. I must admit that those who had already joined spoke in glowing terms about their prospects – free food, free lodgings, free uniform – all this and you got paid for being in the army too. You would also be trained to be a skilled soldier and you would have the camaraderie of a group of blokes your same age.

More and more people we knew were joining up and my younger brother George joined fairly early on. There even became a bit of a feeling that you weren't doing your duty to King and country if you didn't join up and those who chose to stay at home weren't exactly regarded as cowards but they didn't have the hero status of those who did.

I Join The Army.

In October 1914 they formed a new battalion of the Bedfordshire Regiment and the pressure to join around the Baldock area was stepped up. There were lots of posters with Lord Kitchener's face glaring out and with his finger pointing towards us with the message, 'Your Country Needs You'. Work was by now slow and was getting increasingly difficult to come by and now that I had five children to feed I decided in the end to go along with quite a few of my mates and join up.

The recruiting office was in Hitchin and a small group of us walked the five miles to put our signatures on pieces of paper and swear our allegiance on the bible. We were in high spirits and having made our minds up we buoyed one another up and sang some of the popular patriotic songs as we did our best to march along the Hitchin Road. We must have looked a rag-bag collection but we were now proud that we would be 'doing our bit' for our King and country and would be helping to keep a free world.

We had a quick medical inspection for what it was worth together with an eyesight test, we filled in a couple of forms and that was it really. Everyone in our little group passed and we were all very pleased with ourselves. We signed up for three years or until the end of the war, which everyone seemed to think would be a relatively short lived affair.

Back in Baldock that evening we all met up at the Chequers for a couple of pints where we all held our heads up high in the public bar. We were proud to be patriots destined to fight against a despicable enemy for freedom and democracy, although if the truth be known we understood little of what it was all about.

A couple of weeks later all those who had signed up received letters telling us to make our way to Royston station in a weeks' time from where we would be taken to our training camp to be prepared for war.

When the big day arrived my mates and me met outside the Chequers and after a few tearful goodbyes we set off walking the eight miles to Royston. When we got to the station there were what seemed to be hundreds and hundreds of recruits all of who were destined to make up the newly formed Eighth Battalion of the Bedfordshire Regiment.

There was a lot of light-hearted banter on the platform, mainly as a result of general nervousness and not knowing quite what to expect. Eventually though we were all loaded into a very long train with more than the normal number of carriages and I remember we had to walk down the track to get onboard as the train was much longer than the platform. The officers we noted were all comfortably seated in first class whereas we had to make do with third class and were crammed in together like sardines in a tin – we didn't care though, this was the beginning of our great adventure and we eventually set off in high spirits on our way towards London.

Our train journey involved going back through Baldock where I was able to look out of the window to our right and just about see the village of Bygrave where I had spent much of my childhood. The woods and fields had a glow to them in the winter sunshine – something I had never appreciated before when I lived there. It was the epitome of the rural English countryside – rolling fields divided up by hedges, small woods and copses and tiny farms and cottages dotted around with smoke drifting upwards from their chimneys.

The spire of Saint Mary's church came into view soon after as we slowed down to pass through Baldock station. I could see the Chequers pub only a couple of hundred yards from the station and our cottage just behind it – the damp roof slates were glistening and there was smoke rising from their chimney too. I fully expected to be back home before too long but little did I know that this was to be the last time that I would set eyes on my home town.

Just after we had passed Welwyn station we went through two long tunnels and we had to jump up to close the carriage windows as the black smoke from the engine was billowing into the compartment. We were plunged into darkness and everyone coughed and spluttered until the window was eventually closed.

The first part of our journey came to an end at Kings Cross station where we were formed up into columns under the grand canopy that covered the platforms and we then marched across London to Victoria station. Although many of us were out of step and we weren't lined up very well no one said anything as we were doing our best and having had no training as yet I suppose that they couldn't expect much better from us.

On the way we passed down The Mall and proudly marched across the front of Buckingham Palace where we hoped that King George the Fifth might just be looking out of one of the many windows and see us.

From Victoria station we were soon in another train and crossing over the mighty River Thames – at least it was a mighty river to me as I'd never seen anything so wide and fast flowing in my life – I was also impressed with the scale and the sheer number of bridges that were spanning the river.

 The train trundled on to our final destination at Brighton where our initial training was to take place. Here we saw literally thousands of soldiers and raw recruits just like us and they were all anxious to get trained and start fighting the war proper.

We were billeted in large rows of brick built barracks, although some were less fortunate and ended up in tents as there were far more volunteers than there were beds to accommodate them. Apparently Lord Kitchener had hoped to raise one hundred thousand men with his recruitment campaign but as it turned out more than half a million came forward.

After we had been issued with our uniforms and equipment we felt like real soldiers but as we were soon to find out, we had a lot to learn before we could be considered fit to face the enemy.

At first the sheer weight of all our equipment made it difficult to move around. We were issued with good solid hobnail boots, which made a loud sound as we marched along. Woollen puttees came almost up to our knees and we were soon to find that these were the first things that became wet and they then kept our legs wet for long periods of time.

The khaki woollen shirts were very itchy to start with but we soon got used to them and they did at least keep us warm, they were so thick. Over this we had a khaki tunic with a heavy canvas belt. A series of canvas straps clipped to the belt and went over our shoulders to clip on the belt again at the back.

Attached to the belt itself was a felt covered water bottle, a bayonet in a scabbard and an entrenching tool that we would be using to dig trenches when there were no bigger shovels to be had.

We had a haversack and a pack from which hung the mess tin. A waterproof groundsheet would be rolled up and strapped to the top of the pack.

Normally we would carry our overcoat in the pack with extra socks, more underwear and a holdall in which there were such things as our knife, fork and spoon. We also had a button cleaning kit and a 'housewife' for carrying out repairs to our uniforms.

They thoughtfully issued us with writing paper, a pencil, envelopes, our paybook and boot cleaning brushes and dubbin. We had oil and pullthroughs for our rifles.

Finally there were our 'iron rations'; tins of corned beef, biscuits, tea, sugar and Oxo cubes.

Although we only spent a short time in Brighton, just to get ourselves kitted out and issued with all our equipment, the place seemed like a fairy-tale town to me. I was awe struck by the magnificent pier and I couldn't work out how they could have possibly built such a massive structure out into the sea.

On an afternoon off I wandered down to see the Royal Pavilion and was totally spellbound – it was like nothing I had ever seen before. Onion-like roofs, lots and lots of arches and tall decorated chimneys – I'd worked as a bricklayer but I couldn't even begin to think how such complicated and beautiful structures had been created. I was impressed by the large Georgian houses that seemed to make up most of the town – no tiny little cottages here like the ones I'd lived in for the whole of my life.

In all we spent seven months training, most of the time at Woking where we moved to after our short spell at Brighton but occasionally for brief periods at other camps in the south of England.

We soon settled into a routine during our first few weeks of training. The bugle would sound 'reveille' each morning at half past five and we would get up and tidy our things before having a brew. At half past six we would go out on the parade ground for an hour and a half to do various exercises to increase our general level of fitness.

Our fitness session was followed by breakfast after which the rest of the morning would be spent drilling, marching up and down and learning to obey all the routine commands; about turn, right wheel, left wheel, form fours, quick march and halt.

At one o'clock we would knock off for lunch and then more drill during the afternoon until about half past four at which time we were 'off duty'. Of course, if you were unlucky you might have to do fatigues, (some dirty job or other), but usually we were set to clean up our equipment. Polishing our boots until we could see our faces in them, shining up the buttons on our tunics and generally getting everything clean and ship-shape.

At first we didn't have proper rifles to drill with and just had dummy wooden rifles instead – we weren't too pleased about that but we were told that they had been surprised at how many volunteers had come forward to join up and they just didn't have enough arms to go around for the time being.

After a while we did get proper guns and then we started doing night operations and route marches, which we found particularly exhausting. Once we had the rifles we were taught how to handle them and to strip them down and clean them and we practised marksmanship on the ranges.

Learning to fire a rifle proved to be less easy than I had thought, so much kickback on the shoulder and much more noise than I had thought, God knows what it will be like with hundreds going off at the same time.

We practised bayoneting sacks of straw that hung on gallows-like structures and had to shout out loud and make as much noise as possible as we stuck the bayonet into the sack. This was all a bit of a laugh really but in the back of our minds we couldn't help but wonder just how different it would be if we had to stick a bayonet into a real German and how we would feel afterwards.

Much of our time was spent learning how to dig trenches and preparing for trench warfare and we soon realised that we would no doubt be spending many days in these furrows in the earth with little comfort and not much space to move around.

We sometimes went to other camps to train and often we took over public buildings that had been commandeered to accommodate us – schools, town halls and the like. These places weren't usually equipped with beds and so we had to kip down on the floor. We were issued with two blankets and a groundsheet so you can understand that getting some shuteye wasn't always that easy. We weren't given any pillows and we would improvise a pillow by putting our boots inside a haversack.

Before long we thought that we had been taught enough and were itching to get off to wherever the action was – we were never told exactly where we would be going to but the general rumour was that most of the war effort was being fought in Flanders – none of us really knew where that was but it didn't matter, we just wanted to be off.

Our Battalion acquired the nickname of the 'Hungry Eighth' as we were by now all hungry to see something of the real war.

Off To War.

Eventually the day arrived, 29th August 1915, when we were told that we would be moving out the next day to go off to join the great war effort. In fact the war had by now been going on for a year – little did we know that it was a long, long way from being at an end.

We were taken by train down to the docks at Folkestone tucked under the cliffs where we were to board a large ship that was to take us across the English Channel to the French port of Boulogne. The sheer height of the ship with two great big funnels overwhelmed me – we were all dwarfed as we formed ranks on the quayside in the shadow of the great beast.

I looked across the Channel and could just about make out the French coastline; a foreign land – I had no idea of what to expect. My life so far had never brought me into contact with anyone who wasn't English but this was all part of the appeal about what we were doing – the great adventure, see the world, get experience, support the Empire, keep Europe free.

This was the first time that I had been on the sea, my first time on a boat of any description in fact and my first visit abroad. Life in the army was looking good and we were most of us relishing all these new experiences and to cap it all we were getting paid and they were feeding us very well. The training had been hard, especially learning to obey commands without hesitation but we knew now that we were at least superbly fit and could march for miles on end without getting tired.

The crossing to France took about three hours in all and although the sea was calm and the sun was shining, there were many among our number hanging over the side of the ship being seasick – those of us who weren't seasick made fun of them of course.

I made my way towards the front of the boat to be able to see the detail of the coastline of France at the earliest possible moment – as it was a clear day it wasn't long before I could make out the cliffs and houses on the shore ahead. To be quite honest it looked very much the same as the English coast but I wasn't really very sure of just what I was expecting.

Before leaving the ship we were issued with our tin helmets, a nice warm sheepskin coat, gloves and a rubber waterproof cape.

Disembarkation seemed to take forever as there were so many men to be assembled and directed down the two narrow, rickety gangplanks and onto the quayside. We were like a swarm of ants setting foot on the soil of Europe to save them all – I thought that the Germans would have no chance against so many of us.

Eventually we were formed up in ranks alongside the ship and after what seemed like an eternity we marched off towards the railway station.

Along the way the streets were dotted with bedraggled looking French peasants, they looked sad and beaten but they waved to us and occasionally cheered us as we marched past. We felt very proud to be the army that was coming here to save Europe from the aggressor and we held our heads up high and did our best to march like the group of elite professional soldiers we thought we were.

I was intrigued by the local signs on the walls of the little bars we passed, they advertised drinks and cigarettes that I'd never heard of and the smell of the country seemed somehow different from England. Every Frenchman wore a beret, not a cap or trilby like we did at home. The women all wore full striped skirts, aprons and either headscarves of in some cases tall black hats like witches wear.

Once again we boarded a train that took us towards the south east and although our destination was never revealed to us it turned out to be Merville which was a few miles to the west of a large city called Lille. In the past couple of weeks we had been moved around by train quite a bit and this extended my experience as before I'd joined the army I had only been on a train once when I went with Ellen Mary to Royston market for the day; about eight miles from Baldock.

We stayed at Merville for about a couple of weeks and during that time we were billeted in some public offices that had been taken over for our use. Again we had to sleep on the hard unyielding floor and each day we would practise bayonet work and marching back and forth until we were as fit as racehorses.

We were rather crowded in our accommodation but we had decent food and didn't go hungry so we were all happy and still keen to get on with the job in hand.

On 21st September 1915 we were asked to assemble during the afternoon and we marched off leaving Merville behind. We marched for twenty-one miles in all until we arrived at Radinghem at half past two in the morning of the next day very tired and by now pretty hungry as our rations on the way had been fairly scant. We put up tents and rested until the afternoon when at five o'clock we were underway once again marching all through the night until we came to the small village of Molinghem at three in the morning, a total march of eighteen miles. Again we rested during the day and were off again at five in the afternoon; this time we only had to go about five miles to La Miquellerie. Such a short march seemed to be quite a luxury for us.

We stayed at this little village for a whole day taking a well needed rest and were able to clean ourselves up from the mud and sweat that made us feel dirty and uncomfortable.

On the evening of the 24th September we set off once again and reached Bethune, a good-sized town, in the early hours of the morning. Violent thunderstorms raged all through the night and we made our way through mud and running water. We had been told to take extra rations with us as the cookers would be delayed and would probably not catch up with us for a while. This was not good news as we were marching long distances most days and needed to replenish with hot food when we stopped.

The countryside around here was pretty much flat and was obviously a coal mining region as there were lots of high metal towers which I was told were the lifting mechanisms for the cages going down underground to the coal faces – we didn't have anything at all like that around Baldock. On the surface were high slagheaps that formed the only relief from the naturally flat ground. We had been told that warfare in flat terrain would be particularly dangerous as the enemy would have a clear sight of our approach and there would be little cover from their firepower. On the other hand it would also be easier for us to see them coming and be able to pick them off.

Our progress was slowed down by the sheer volume of military traffic on the roads and every now and then we had to stop at level crossings to allow long trains full of armaments to pass by. The trains were mainly carrying great big guns and we felt that the enemy would surely be easily beaten with such weapons against them. All the roads were badly churned up and were heavily rutted and swimming with mud.

Rumour had it that a big push was coming up and we were to be a part of it. This was later to be known as the Battle of Loos, which is pronounced 'Loss'. We didn't know it at the time but it was the biggest battle that the British forces had been engaged in thus far in the war.

 We knew by now that we were getting close to the area where the real fighting was taking place, as there was a continual roar of big artillery guns throughout the day. Whether they were our guns or the enemy's we didn't know.

We were billeted in the Girl's College in Bethune and had a bit more comfort than we had been used to over the past week when we had been on the move. Our rest though didn't last very long as we were ordered to move on that same afternoon.

We ended up at a place called Fosse No. 9 which was right on the battlefront. Now we had our first real experience of the trenches. As it had been raining almost non-stop for several days the majority of the trenches were flooded out, sometimes up to our knees or even above. There were wooden duckboards in most of the trenches but generally the water was at least a foot above them.

Although the front walls of the trenches were sandbagged with a small step up or firestep at the bottom, the rear walls were generally simply muddy earth cut at a slight angle and as it rained the water cascaded down the wall. You can imagine therefore that just walking or running through the trenches covered you with mud and your clothes were continuously soaking wet with nowhere and no time to dry them out.

Just before six in the morning our side had let off a large number of chlorine gas containers, the first time that the British had used gas.

The idea with the gas was that the wind would take it across to the German lines. Some five thousand nine hundred cylinders of gas had been set up in front of our trenches the night before but what wind there had been had dropped by the time the cylinders were set off and most of the gas just hung in the air as a menacing cloud and failed to reach the German lines. The greenish-yellow smoke hung heavy in the air and formed a cloud about forty feet or so high.

We even heard later on that in some places along the front the wind changed direction and blew the gas back onto the British lines with quite a few casualties some of whom we were to come into contact with later on.

We noticed that our buttons would turn green whenever we were exposed to the gas and the only good thing about it was that it certainly got the rats running out of their holes and scampering for cover.

We did at least get some warning when there was gas around and at first this was by means of a series of rattles, a bit like the ones at football matches, situated at intervals along the trenches. Later on though these were replaced by Strombos horns, which were much louder and sounded like foghorns.

At about eight o'clock on the morning of the 25th September we were ordered to go forward towards the enemy lines from our own trenches. We weren't too sure of exactly what we were supposed to do as this was our first experience of the real thing.

The 9th Suffolks and the 11th Essex had made an earlier assault and we were to provide support for them. By now we realised that most of the artillery fire we were hearing was in fact our own which was being directed over our heads to the second line of German trenches, intended to soften them up before we made our attack.

We crossed no man's land without too much trouble as our previous artillery fire had successfully broken through most of the barbed wire and we arrived at the German front line trenches to find that they had been evacuated, which to be quite honest was a bit of a relief.

We pressed on towards the German second line of trenches but came under intense machine-gun fire and there were still many shells coming across and I was aware of men falling on either side of me.

As the shells whipped through the sky above us with a screeching whine we tried to take cover by diving into the many shell holes on the way but fell into the seething layer of stinking mud, water and slime in the bottom of the holes. Some of the shell holes had dead bodies in them and we found ourselves falling on top of them in an effort to get below the line of sight of the machine gunners.

As the shells fell around us we pressed ourselves into the very earth as plumes of soil, mud and stones were thrown high into the air.

There was insufficient safe cover for us and men were being mown down all along the line of advance so we received the order to fall back to the first line of the German trenches that we had just left and then subsequently to our own from where we had started several hours before.

By three o'clock on the morning of the 26th September we were again in the front line of our own trenches and we were again in support of the Norfolks who were launching an attack on an area known as the Quarries just a bit to the north west of the town of Hulloch.

The morning was thick with mist and fog – very damp and with a chill in the air. Our breath came out of our mouths like smoke and our wet uniforms were steaming from the heat of our bodies.

As we pressed on we came across a series of trenches that were occupied by the Cameron Highlanders who told us they knew nothing of the whereabouts of the Norfolks who we were supposed to be backing up.

Moving on we came across more abandoned trenches and we jumped down into them to find a horrific sight of many dead British bodies and lots of wounded too. One of the Highlanders had been caught up on the bared wire in no mans land and his corpse hung there like a scarecrow dangling in the air.

The stretcher-bearers were already there but had great difficulty in moving through the trenches as there were so many bodies around.

It was sickening to see the corpses of our dead comrades, many without arms or legs and some blown nearly to pieces. Among these heaps of dead there lay writhing in the blood-stained mud those who had been seriously injured but had survived. It seemed an impossible task for the relatively few stretcher-bearers to get these severely injured men back to a place of safety. Many were surely doomed to die a terrible slow and painful death in the most ghastly conditions imaginable.

Being subjected to three hours of continual rifle and shellfire and gas attacks we were unable to get any news of the Norfolks and so made our way back to our front line trenches. There were many other units in our trenches and we became rather mixed up and separated from our mates. Communication was more or less non-existent between the various battalions and even our own officers sometimes had difficulty in passing commands along the line as the noise of the gunfire was usually tremendous.

At about six in the evening we were relieved by the Coldstream Guards and we pulled back to Vermelles where we bivouacked for the night. The next morning the cookers and supplies caught up with us and we were able to have a hot meal, the first one for more than twenty-four hours.

It was now our turn to pull back having served our time at the front and we moved back to Noeux les Mines a mile or so back from Vermelles. Our attack had come to nothing and very little ground had been gained; in fact in some places along the front no advance had been made at all.

On our way back away from the front line we walked alongside long columns of wounded who were making their way back to the field hospitals for treatment, some of them walking with assistance from a comrade and other being wheeled along on barrows.

The roads had been cleared to allow the free movement of troops and vehicles and it was horrific to see the number of dead bodies that had simply been pushed to the side of the road forming heaps of decaying soldiers covered with hundreds of black flies.

We were now returned to behind the lines and we set up our tents in the pouring rain, it had been raining all day and we were thoroughly soaked – it was by now the end of September and along with the almost continual rain it was getting colder each day. Nevertheless we were pleased to be out of the front line trenches and away from the very real risk of getting killed.

No sooner had we got the tents set up and were looking forward to getting some sleep when we were ordered to break camp and we were marched off to nearby Nouex les Mines railway station where we were put on a train and taken up to Berguette station and from there we marched on to Ham en Artois where we arrived just after two o'clock in the morning, once again soaking wet and dog tired.

We spent the night in some old farm buildings which although draughty were at least reasonably dry and that was better than having to put the tents up again as the canvas they were made from was by now heavy with water and covered with mud. We however were soaked to the skin and had to turn in as we were, as there was nowhere to get dry and clean ourselves – fortunately we were so tired that it didn't really matter. Rest and sleep was our first priority.

We were able to sleep until the afternoon and then marched five miles to Norrent Fontes where we took over billets from the 12th Royal Fusiliers. The next day was spent in giving our equipment and ourselves a well needed scrub.

After a couple of days of relative rest we were once again on the move marching back to Berguette where again we found a train waiting to take us on to Godewarsvelde which was up near the Belgian border.

Once we had all grouped together we crossed over the border on foot and continued for seven miles or so to the village of Watou; the billeting officer met us there and took us on to two farms just to the north east of the village. Our accommodation there was the best that we had had as yet, dry barns and lots of clean straw to sleep on and we hoped that we might be staying there for a bit.

In fact we only stayed at the farms for a couple of days, cleaning equipment and continuing our training before we moved on about ten miles to Vlamertinghe.

It was still pouring with rain as about three hundred of us were put up in either farm buildings or tents. We were now very close to the town of Ypres, which everyone referred to as 'Wipers' as it was a lot easier for us English to pronounce. Ypres has seen a lot of action over the past few months and was to see a lot more in the coming weeks.

The town, which I reckon had once been a very nice place, was in ruins – many of the buildings were raised to the ground, others were half demolished and the roads were a complete mess. Most of the locals had moved out but a few had stayed on and were glad to see us although we couldn't help but think that our presence would cause further destruction to the town.

Most of the dead had been cleared away from the town but occasionally you would see a body or two and this gave the town a ghoulish atmosphere.

Before we went back to the real fighting in the front line trenches we helped transport a large group of casualties to a nearby temporary hospital. As well as those suffering from gunshot and shrapnel wounds there were quite a few who had been exposed to gas, both ours and that of the Germans.

We were deploying gas now on a regular basis and it seemed to me to be a fairly dodgy procedure. Hundreds of gas cylinders would be lined up ahead of the front line trenches during the night and then set off in the morning if the wind was in the right direction to take the gas over no mans land and into the German front line trenches.

As this business with the gas was a relatively new thing we hadn't been issued with gas masks and we had to make do when there was gas in the air by improvising a makeshift mask with pieces of cloth soaked in water. It was said that they were supposed to be more effective if you peed on the cloth rather than use water. Either way I didn't find it very effective and you ended up coughing and spewing up all over the place.

The poor sods that we took to the hospital would be coughing their guts up and spitting out a foul greenish froth from their lungs. They complained of splitting headaches, a knife-like pain in the lungs and they all had a dreadful thirst. Apparently they weren't allows to drink anything as this would have meant instant death for some reason. The colour of their skin was a greenish, yellowy black and their eyes seemed to have a vacant stare about them.

We were now moved back to the trenches where I must admit the fighting wasn't quite as intense as we had experienced before but we were still losing a couple of men each day, mainly to snipers when some silly bugger put his head up above the top of the trench. There were normally periscopes for looking over the top into no mans land and beyond but these were usually covered with mud and it was always difficult to get a clear view through the mirrors. This meant that it was often quicker and easier to pop your head over the parapet for a look although sometimes with fatal consequences.

As October wore on the rain kept on lashing down and the temperature started to drop even further so we were getting frosts during the night. Now, not only were we continually soaked through up to our knees and covered in mud, but our feet and legs were also freezing cold. It was difficult to fire a gun with frozen fingers and taking a good aim wasn't so easy when you were shaking and shivering violently with the cold.

Much of our day was spent pumping water out of the trenches, digging them deeper and rebuilding the sides and supporting them with sandbags. In some places the trenches had collapsed completely as the sides had been turned into liquid mud by the torrential rain.

The pools of water in the bottom of the trenches were alive with small frogs and large red slugs crawled up the muddy sides. There were also a lot of queer looking beetles with dangerous looking horns that would wriggle their way along the dry ledges and into the dugouts.

The dugouts were really just small chambers dug into the rear walls of the trench and reinforced with bits of timber to stop them from collapsing – they were reserved for the officers and senior N.C.O.s. Us 'other ranks' had to make do with 'pozzies' which were just small holes in the walls and unsupported. They were damp and muddy inside but if it was raining really heavily they were marginally better than standing outside trying to wrap a rubber cape around your body and getting drenched to the skin. They did give you the impression that you were an animal cringing in a burrow though. These 'pozzies' were banned after a while on account of the number of cave-ins when quite a few men were buried alive.

Our normal routine was to spend eight days in the front line trenches followed by another eight days in the reserve trenches which were a bit further back but no less prone to shelling and then sixteen days in the nearest town billets behind the lines. Although even this wasn't that safe for if a German aircraft spotted us you could bet that they would direct their artillery fire onto us. The spotter aircraft even dropped bombs on us on one occasion but we survived.

When we were in the billets in a town or village we did have the chance to frequent the local 'estaminets', which were very rough and ready places and the local equivalent of our English pub. Here we were able to buy wine or sometimes beer and if we wanted to try something a bit different to our boring army rations then they would serve up omelettes for us, which was something that we hadn't come across before, or if we could afford it then the owner would usually be able to rustle up a steak and chips.

Most of our pay, which was recorded in our pay-books, was allocated and paid to our families back in England, but the rest we received in the local currency francs, and we could spend this in the villages as we wished.

By the end of November 1915 we had been moved back to Poperinghe to yet another wet, muddy camp. The only good thing about this was that we now had a chance to take a bath. One Sunday there was a church service in the local cinema which was attended by pretty much all of the men, not so much for religious reasons but more because it was relatively warm, dry and comfortable – I saw that a few of the men fell asleep during the service.

Our training continued every day although by now we were getting some really cold, hard frosts.

On the 3rd December we started off on a route march but we were ordered to stop about halfway to be inspected by General Plumer who was the Commander of the Second Army.

The very next day our billets were inspected by Brigadier General Nicholson - so much top brass all of a sudden. That night though the wind got up and was blowing so hard that it blew down a number of walls in the Transport Section and nine horses were buried under the rubble – we all got stuck in digging them out but three of the poor things had died by the time we got to them.

The trenches were still deep in water but now there was often a thin layer of ice on it in the morning as we kept up our pumping duties. The water we were pumping out had bits of bodies in it, clotted blood and a covering of metallic greenish slime from the gas bombs.

After we had pumped out most of the water it was sometimes necessary to dig out the bottom of the trench to make it deeper so our heads didn't show above the parapet. I remember once when we were doing this we dug into a rotting body – one of our mates – not a nice job.

Having by now spent several months in and out of the trenches during which time our feet and legs had rarely been dry, many of us were developing 'trench foot'. If you got this your feet would swell up to two or three times their normal size and go completely dead – you could stick a knife into them and not feel a thing. After a while the swelling would go down and it was then that the most indescribable agony would begin. During the night you could hear men screaming out loud with the pain and they sometimes ended up having their feet amputated.

One thing that by now we had more or less taken for granted was the presence of lice on our bodies. It became a daily ritual to try to keep their numbers down by stripping off our clothes and scraping the little sods out of the seams and folds of our clothes with the back of a knife. The fact that it was very cold and our clothes were always soaking wet and sticking to our bodies didn't help at all as we were reluctant to strip off too much and get even colder.

We weren't allowed to light fires to keep warm as the smoke would have given away our position to the enemy and they would have been able to range their guns in on our trenches. The absence of fires meant that we were continually cold night and day and sleep was difficult to come by although we were always dog-tired.

The only places we could sleep were on the duckboards at the bottom of the trench or on the muddy firestep below the parapet and we used to huddle together to get a bit of warmth from one another's bodies. I must admit that it seemed a bit strange to cuddle up to another bloke but if you didn't you would shiver violently all night and not sleep at all.

Huddling together did however have the disadvantage of encouraging the lice to spread from one man to another but it was the only way we could get at least a few minutes sleep at night and that was about all we could expect.

During the winter of 1915 we spent most of our time either at Poperinghe or Ypres although we never seemed to make much progress in terms of territory gained. We would make a big effort and maybe make a couple of hundred yards and then the Germans would retaliate and take back the ground we had taken. This backwards and forwards went on all winter and no one ever seemed to get the upper hand but all the time more and more men on both sides were being killed on a daily basis.

On the 17th March 1916 just as the weather was beginning to improve we were marched off to the station once again and we were entrained to Calais up on the coast of France for what turned out to be a bit of a holiday for us. We spent the time under canvas at Beaumaris Camp. General Plumer made the odd appearance now and again and we spent the best part of a week drilling and marching on the beach which was a really nice change for us – we could even go for a swim in the sea so our bodies were cleaner than they had been for quite a while.

One day they even organised a sports day for us when we were encouraged to run races, play football and generally have a good time.

After a couple of weeks though, we were back on the train to Poperinghe and back into the same old routine. For most of the month of April we were at the Yser Canal bank where we suffered some heavy casualties, a hundred and thirty men killed and sixty-five wounded on the night of the 19th/20th alone. The Germans made some ground and took over our trenches but we got them back again the next day with the help of the Kings Own Shropshire Light Infantry.

Later on in May some of the men were even presented with cards acknowledging their acts of gallantry and devotion to duty on the night of the 19th.

We were inoculated a few days later – I don't know what it was to prevent but we got a day off afterwards – and a week or so later we had to have the second dose and another day off. After what we were going through the effects of a little inoculation was nothing but we didn't complain about the days off.

The summer of 1916 wore on with much more rain than I would have expected. This kept us busy with pumping operations and rebuilding the sides of the trenches with sandbags. When the rain did eventually stop, you won't believe it but we had a spell of very hot weather and many of us found it difficult to cope with after the miserable conditions we had become used to. Lots of the men suffered from sunburn but this received little sympathy from the officers who told them that is was self-inflicted.

We Move to the Somme.

On the 2nd August we were moved back into France with rumours once again that something big was about to happen – to be quite honest we were so tired and worn out that we just followed orders and although it was nice to think that we wouldn't be stuck in the same old place our future was out of our hands and no one really told us anything.

We were taken in yet another train to the station at the small village of Amplier, which was near to Doullens where our first job was to guard a group of German prisoners. We couldn't speak to any of them as none of us knew German and none of them spoke English. They were a sorry looking bedraggled bunch, most of them seemed to be very young but you got the feeling that they were glad to be out of the fighting but were a bit worried as to what was going to happen to them – I think they thought that we were going to shoot them. It was strange to see the enemy up close in person and to see that to all intents and purposes they were pretty much like us.

We were marched around from one place to another but still away from the front lines. Training took place every day, kit was cleaned and we almost enjoyed not having to grovel around in mud and filth and not to have to worry about getting your head shot off if you were a bit careless or being blown to pieces by an enemy shell landing alongside you in the trench.

The 30th August marked one year since we had been in Europe and it rained once again very heavily and constantly throughout the day. The date was noted but there was no celebration – we just wondered how much longer it would all go on for and whether or not we as individuals would live to see the end of the war.

The area we were now in was near the River Somme although we never did get to see the river itself. The land was generally very flat with just a few minor rolling hills here and there. It had obviously been a farming region, not entirely unlike the north of Hertfordshire, but you wouldn't have known that by the time we arrived there because of the damage that had been inflicted on the countryside.

By the first week in September we had moved up close to the village of Maricourt, which was a few miles east of Albert and we were back in the trenches once again. Most of the trenches here had seen a lot of continuous action over the past year as was evidenced by the large amount of rubbish around.

Most of our rations came in tins; bully-beef, stew, pork and beans, jam, biscuits, etcetera, most of which were made in Scotland by a firm with the unlikely name of Maconochie's. My favourite was the stew, which was usually served with a few vegetables and if we were lucky some bread.

As there was no means of disposing of rubbish the empty tins would be thrown over the top of the trench and over a period of time they had built up in layers a foot or so deep in some places.

All these tins with remnants of food in them were a good source of food for the rats. I'd seen plenty of rats around Baldock as there were quite a few maltings in the town belonging to Simpson's brewery. Maltings meant lots of grain lying around and there were always rats to be seen, but they were always very cautious, timid creatures and would run off at the first sight of man.

Here in France though the rats seemed to have little or no fear. They were always in and out of the trenches looking for food – more than once I woke up from my makeshift bed on the floor of the trench to find a rat running across my chest.

If you had even a scrap of food in your pocket they would climb inside to look for it. Several men had been bitten by the rats when they had tried to hit them of shoo them away.

One of the eeriest sensations was at night on those rare occasions when there was no gunfire and everything was relatively quiet. We would sit huddled in the bottom of the trench listening to the constant rustling sound of the discarded tins as the rats foraged through them eating the remnants of food.

The most sickening sight though was when we had to go out into no mans land to pick up the dead bodies of our colleagues and those survivors who were too badly injured to make it back on their own. Sometimes as we picked up dead bodies a rat would shoot out of the poor victim's mouth – I suppose the rats found it easier to eat the soft parts inside the body rather than have to chew through the outer flesh.

Some of the badly injured told of how they had to fight off the rats as they lay there unable to move as the hideous creatures tried to eat them alive. It's surprising that we didn't contract more diseases than we did.

The smell of rotting food and decaying bodies was always with us as it would often be days before it was safe enough for us to venture out of the trenches to bring back the dead. This stench of death was added to by the smell of the latrines – these were in little side trenches off the main ones where shallow holes had been dug in which to do our business – you can imagine with so many men crammed into the trenches these holes soon filled up and overflowed and the smell was awful.

The latrine trenches were often not so deep and the enemy could sometimes get sight of anyone using them

– their snipers would often range in on the latrines and some of the men would choose to relieve themselves elsewhere in an old helmet or a used food tin to avoid getting shot.

It was something that we just had to get used to but it wasn't easy to put it all to the back of your mind and there was no way of getting the smell out of your nostrils.

On the 12th September 1916 we moved up to other trenches near the village of Ginchy just to the side of Leuze Wood, although you would never have known that it had been a wood. With so much shelling and gunfire across the area the trees had all been stripped back to charred stumps – every vestige of leaves and branches had gone and these stumps stuck up out of the ground which was full of flooded, mud-filled shell holes. There was nothing but brown earth, tree stumps, shell holes and death all around us.

In the lulls between the firing there was absolute silence – no sound of any birds or other animals, not even a sparrow in the sky. Where had all the birds gone I wondered – to a better place than this surely.

Not only were there no living creatures to be seen, but there were no living plants either. The trees were all shot up and the bullets and shells had stripped the branches bare and the earth itself was devoid of anything that even slightly resembled a plant – no grass, no weeds, no flowers; no green, no colours, just barren, dead brown earth.

Of course the shell holes quickly filled with rainwater and became muddy hellholes that were often the only place to dive for cover when we were trying to move forward across the relatively flat ground. You never knew what you would be diving into when you did this as there were often bits of bodies and rotting flesh in the bottom of the craters not to mention pieces of barbed wire and lumps of sharp metal that could be the cause a serious injury.

From our position in the frontline trenches we could easily see the enemy across the other side of what had been a field at some time in what seemed to have been the distant past. Their defensive position was about three or four hundred yards away and those men who we were replacing had been engaged for some time in trying to take this stronghold. It was called the Quadrilateral as it was apparently made up of a series of complicated trenches that roughly formed the shape of a four- sided figure.

The Quadrilateral was slightly higher than our position, not by much, only a few yards really but enough to give the Germans the advantage of being able to see us coming towards them across the open field where our only cover was the shell holes.

By now we knew that there was soon to be a big push in an attempt to break through the enemy lines as more and more troops were being brought in each day. Our particular objective though was to take the Quadrilateral – it wasn't going to be easy.

A new weapon had been developed, the tank, and we had been promised that three of these new wonders would be ready and in place to help us with our assault on the Quadrilateral which was scheduled to take place on 15th September – my birthday!

We were very confident when we thought that we would have tanks to help us as, for as we understood it, they were impregnable metal boxes on tracks that could withstand machine gun fire and they would simply drive across no mans land and fire at the enemy without the Germans being able to do anything about it.

A total of fifty tanks had been shipped over from Britain and assembled in France but none of them made it to where we were. As I understood it most of them either refused to start or broke down shortly after and so as it turned out they wouldn't have been much use to us anyway.

On the morning of the 15th September 1916 we were briefed to be ready and in our positions at 0420 hours for the big attack. Zero hour was 0620 hours and was to be preceded by a heavy artillery bombardment from 0600 hours onwards. Our big guns were situated a long way behind our lines and would fire over the top of us and into the enemy lines in front of us.

We were all ready to go and installed in the front line trenches well before four o'clock – line upon line of us packed in two or three rows deep or as much as the width of the trench would allow.

We now had a two hour wait in the dark before dawn and the call to go over the top – I'd been in this situation many times before and it was always a tense time; a time for reflection and moreover perhaps a time to ponder on what was about to come in the next few hours.

It was pretty obvious that not all of us would live to see the end of the day or perhaps even worse we might get wounded and left to suffer, screaming in pain in the stinking mud and slime among the rats in no man's land.

I had always thought before that 'what will be will be' – as we used to say 'if the bullet has your name on it you're done for; if it doesn't then you live to fight another day'. But today was a bit different and I had a strange feeling in my gut that something momentous was about to happen.

Maybe it was because it was my birthday – thirty-nine years old today.

I thought about Ellen Mary and the children; Billy, (who was by now twelve years old), Frank, (ten years old), Dorothy, (eight years old), Leslie, (four years old) and baby Christobel who was already two years old. The last time I had seen Christobel when I left Baldock she was only four months old, a baby in her mother's arms who wouldn't remember me even if I managed to get back home in one piece.

I thought about Chequers Yard and my Mum and Dad and my brothers and sisters and I wondered what was going on there right at this moment. It was a Friday so they should soon be getting up and going about their various tasks before very long.

Some of the chaps in the line tried to crack jokes or make light-hearted remarks but they were generally ignored as most of us were fully aware of the gravity of the situation.

Four hundred yards away was the Quadrilateral and if we took it today we would be heroes; four hundred yards doesn't seem like much but by the end of today that four hundred yards of stinking mud and shell holes would no doubt be covered with many dead bodies and a lot of blood and bits of flesh – more fodder for the rats.

I reflected on what I'd left behind, our close knit family group in the two cottages at the back of the Chequers pub – nothing fancy but it was warm by the fire in the winter and warm out in the courtyard in the summer sunshine. Sometimes it had been hard going when there was not much work to be had but what I now remembered was the dryness and comfort of it all compared to what I'd had to put up with for the past year or so. Wet feet, wet legs, sodden wet uniform, grovelling round most days in mud and water, pumping water out of the trenches and leaning against muddy trench walls. All this together with being infested with lice and living hand in glove with rats, all manner of creepy crawly insects and big orange slugs that would crawl over your body if you gave them a chance.

The plan for the day was that the artillery would continue shelling the enemy lines right up until the last moment – twenty minutes of continuous and unrelenting bombardment -we would then get across to their lines as fast as we possibly could before they had time to recover their positions.

In the event, the shelling by our artillery stopped well short of 0620 hours – no one knew why and the officers were obviously reluctant to blow the whistle in case the artillery started up again and we got caught in the fire. We waited in the ensuing silence until zero hour before going over the top and during this time there had been no more shelling. The eastern sky was now beginning to show signs of light as the sun was about to break out above the horizon.

This long pause no doubt gave the Germans plenty of time to get back into their positions and in particular to man their machine gun emplacements which was no doubt to be our biggest danger of the day.

The whistle blew and we were off. Just getting out of the trench was difficult enough with the mud all around us as not all of us were close enough to the makeshift wooden scaling ladders, which did make the task of getting out of the trench somewhat easier.

The first thing that I noticed was that the three or four hundred yards between us and the enemy was still heavily covered with barbed wire, not all of which had been destroyed by our earlier shelling. This meant that we had to cut our way through the wire in many places and we were consequently often held up in one position giving the enemy an easier target.

When we were about half way to the Quadrilateral the German machine gun fire started up and I could see the bullets from their guns sweeping across the field ahead of me. I threw myself down into a mud-filled shell hole. Alongside me an officer waved his pistol in the air and signalled for us to continue our advance.

We dodged from one shell hole to another and could hear the pieces of shrapnel whizzing through the air and landing with heavy thuds as they hit the ground around us. When the bigger shells landed the earth would shake violently beneath our feet and it felt as if we were about to be swallowed up by an enormous earthquake.

Weighted down now with mud all over my uniform I struggled to my feet and staggered forward once again – I was finding it heavy going and I struggled to get my breath in the cold morning air.

I made a few more yards forward but was conscious of men falling on both sides of me. Some of those who had made faster progress than me fell too and I had to jump over their bodies to continue towards the Quadrilateral.

I looked around to judge just how far we had come when a searing pain shot through my legs and then the machine gun bullets sprayed across my chest and there was blackness.

Epilogue.

The Quadrilateral was not taken on 15th September but did fall to the allied troops three days later on the 18th allowing the allies to advance about one mile.

Frank's body was never identified and it is quite possible that it was never found and still lies today beneath the ground in the field just south of the position of the Quadrilateral and close to the village of Ginchy.

If his body was in fact recovered, then it was almost certainly buried in the nearby Guillemont Road Cemetery along with 2,262 other soldiers; of these some 1,523 are unidentified and have 'Known Unto God' inscribed on their headstones.

On that day in September 1916 over twenty-nine thousand British and Commonwealth troops died during this one offensive – three thousand six hundred of these were from the sixth Division to which the Bedfordshire Regiment was attached.

At High Wood, which is not far from the scene of Frank's death, there are an estimated 8,000 bodies that have never been recovered.

Today the field where Frank died is often planted with wheat which blows and sways casually in the breeze but around the edges of the field are littered dozens of shell cases, some of them still live, which get turned up each year by tractors as the land is ploughed. A gruesome and vivid reminder of those days a hundred years ago when so many lost their lives.

Printed in Germany
by Amazon Distribution
GmbH, Leipzig